W9-APG-486

Thank you for

ENCOUNTERS WITH POLICE:
A Black Man's Guide to Survival

Eric C. Broyles, Esq.
Adrian O. Jackson, Patrolman

your support

DEDICATION

Michael Brown
Oscar Grant
Sean Bell
Eric Garner
Amadou Diallo
Tamir Rice
John Crawford
Timothy Thomas
Jonathan Ferrell

The countless other known and unknown black men and boys who have died during an encounter with police

And

Trayvon Martin

CONTENTS

PREFACE

We are African-American men who have been best friends for over 30 years. One of us tried to burglarize a police station impound lot at the age of 10 and later became an attorney. One of us is a 25-year veteran of a police department in Ohio. We draw on our experiences as a lawyer and as a police officer to give insights to black men and boys on how to get home alive after encountering the police. We dedicate this book to the memories of Michael Brown, John Crawford, Amadou Diallo, Oscar Grant, Timothy Thomas, Eric Garner, Tamir Rice, Jonathan Ferrell and the countless other black men who have died following an encounter with police. We also dedicate this book to the fathers, mothers, aunts, uncles, sisters, brothers, grandparents and other relatives and friends who have lost loved ones following encounters with police.

This book does not prescribe how to solve the broader and deeper social problems that underlie some of the interactions between black boys and men and the police. The deeper social problems need to be addressed. We just don't have the luxury of time to wait for those issues to be effectively dealt with before another black man or boy dies during an encounter with police. What we can fix now is what we do as black men and boys when we have an encounter so that we leave it peacefully. This in no way excuses the police of their responsibility to do their jobs according to the law and without bias. We acknowledge that we can't control what will happen when police officers don't act responsibly and within the law. We can and we must, however, learn to control ourselves in these situations.

FOREWORD

Whenever there is a perceived ambiguity on some social, political, or legal issue, there is one phrase you can count on being uttered by a majority of commentators: "It's not black and white." The problem with that sentiment is that when it comes to interactions involving black men and the police, the end result of an interaction is directly influenced by the race of both parties. What's more troubling than the racial bias that seems to somehow justify the killing of black men, is that more often than not, black men don't survive these encounters.

The 2008 election and 2012 re-election of President Barack Obama, the first African American elected as President of the United States, had many leaders, mentors, and influential people in the black community feeling empowered, motivated, and hopeful that America was finally making a change on its views of black males. Unfortunately, it seems as though his election has not sparked the social change that many expected, and some even argue that things have gotten progressively worse for black men.

The most recent killings of unarmed black men has the black community confused over what they can and should do in order to prevent a trip to a retail store, walking down a street, or breaking up a fight from turning into a deadly encounter with the police. What makes this book special is that it provides a blueprint for doing exactly that. This book separates itself from other attempts to guide black males, because the authors both walk in the shoes of a black man in America, and can provide a perspective as experts of the American legal justice system and police policy and procedures. Read this book, and take what it says to heart, because it could be the difference between making it home for dinner with the ones that you love or having the ones that love you plan your homegoing service.

I have known Eric Broyles for over 25 years. We have laughed, cried, and studied together. His passion for

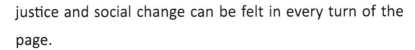

justice and social change can be felt in every turn of the page.

> Michael Wright, Managing Partner
> Wright & Schulte LLC
> Attorney for family of John Crawford

CHAPTER 1:
WE WROTE THIS BOOK FOR YOU

This book is intended to provide a practical guide for black men and boys on how to react when they encounter police in any setting in order to keep the interaction peaceful so that everyone leaves the encounter safely. We recognize that members of other racial and ethnic groups and women have had tragic encounters with police as well. We wrote this book for African-American men because we know their experience best based upon our life lessons and believe they are at greater risk for something bad happening. Furthermore, our suggestions for how to interact with police are race and gender neutral so anyone can apply these principles and survive their own encounters. This book is not intended to be an exhaustive analysis of every social, legal, psychological, or economic issue that arises in this book. This book is a practical step-by-step guide on how to reduce the occurrence of similar deaths in the future. We did not write this book to win a Pulitzer Prize. We wrote this book to help keep you alive

when you encounter police.

My name is Eric Broyles and I am an African-American attorney in Washington, D.C. My path did not start out so promising as I was a juvenile delinquent by the age of 10 and really disliked the police. In fact, my anger and resentment towards police officers motivated me to try to steal a motorized mini-bike from my local police department's impound lot. I was arrested at a young age which intensified my grudge against police. I grew up in the small southwest Ohio city of Hamilton near Cincinnati and during the course of my life I have had at least 20 encounters with police officers either as a suspect, driver, passenger, pedestrian, or bystander. In almost all of those police encounters, I had neutral or positive interactions with the police officers. Aside from my arrest as a juvenile, I can only recall two very negative encounters with police and one in which I feared I might lose my life. I attribute most of my noncontroversial encounters with police to some sage advice that I received from my childhood best friend and now 25-year veteran police officer Adrian

Jackson. Adrian became a police officer in 1989 during my sophomore year of college at the University of Cincinnati. Specifically, he offered me some practical tips on how to interact with police officers in traffic stop situations. Adrian knew that I was spending an inordinate amount of time driving because I worked fulltime selling garage doors to pay my college tuition. As a college student working a fulltime job, I was always rushing trying to meet all of my obligations each day. Consequently, I developed a bad habit of speeding as I drove from sales appointments around Cincinnati; Dayton, Ohio; and northern Kentucky to reach my sales quota before driving back to my college campus library at night to study. I mentioned to Adrian that I was ticketed for speeding while I was rushing from one sales appointment to another. Adrian told me that I needed to slow down and that he understood what I was trying to accomplish with school and work. Adrian said "Eric, I know how hard you are working to pay for your tuition and keep up with your school work, but your driving habits need to change and you need to calm down, especially when police pull you over." He added that "I know you and understand why you drive the way you do, but another police officer does not know you. You need to know what they might be thinking when you get pulled over." Since Adrian was my best friend I really tried to understand what he has to go through as a police officer and began to think about how modest changes to behavior by the public can make encounters with police uneventful. Adrian is my co-author and his advice helped to change my perspective on police and how to avoid threatening contacts with them. We hope this book will help African-American men and boys survive their own encounters with police.

In recent years there has been a spate of violence between police officers and young African-American men and in several of those instances unarmed African-American men were killed. In 2001, in a city just south of where Adrian and I grew up, Cincinnati police officer Stephen Roach shot and killed 19-year old Timothy Thomas during a chase following an attempted arrest. Thomas had a warrant out for his arrest for 14 nonviolent misdemeanor offenses—most of them traffic violations. Thomas's killing by police sparked violent riots in downtown Cincinnati and even led to a boycott of the city by numerous civil rights organizations. More recently, on August 9, 2014 18-year old Michael Brown was shot by Ferguson, Missouri police officer Darren Wilson. Michael Brown's death also sparked massive and sometimes violent protests in Ferguson, Missouri and surrounding areas.

Shortly after the killing, a Ferguson grand jury decided not to indict police officer Darren Wilson for Michael Brown's death and this decision led to nationwide protests and unrest. We understand the anguish and confusion that young black men are feeling. Undoubtedly, anger, fear, and even hopelessness are all feelings that might emerge and we want to encourage you to open your hearts and minds to a different approach to police that actually gives you power. We want to offer a perspective here not to defend police misconduct, but to keep this misconduct in perspective as most police officers do not kill members of the public. We offer a different way of thinking about police and who they are. We offer simple, straightforward steps. With these steps, no matter what leads you to your encounter with police, we believe that you will be safe. We also show you where your true power resides and it is not in overreacting in the moment. Your true power lies in other venues available to all citizens to redress police misconduct. However, you have to be alive to participate in those other avenues such as testifying before a grand jury. We did not hear Trayvon Martin telling his side of the story about when he encountered George Zimmerman nor could we hear Michael Brown's story about when he encountered Officer Darren Wilson. We are saddened that 18-year old Michael Brown lost his life. We are frustrated that we did not get to hear his story. *You deserve to be heard.* We want your voice to be heard and for you to at least have a chance to have a different outcome than those who were not heard following their encounters with police.

Michael Brown's family attorneys, who were also

the attorneys for Trayvon Martin's family, have been friends of mine for nearly 20 years. Attorneys Ben Crump and his law partner--and my fraternity brother--Daryl Parks have become the go-to attorneys for these types of tragedies. When Ben Crump and Daryl Parks and I met in Tallahassee, Florida in 1995 shortly after each of us had taken the bar exam in our respective states, I doubt any of us imagined that they would focus a large part of their legal careers on addressing unthinkable killings of young black men. When we met, I had just moved to Tallahassee, Florida to begin a prestigious judicial clerkship on the United States Court of Appeals for the Eleventh Circuit.[1] Ben Crump and Daryl Parks had just launched their law practice in the city where they attended both college and law school. They welcomed me to their city and we have been friends ever since. About a week after a Florida jury acquitted George Zimmerman of charges for killing of Trayvon Martin, I ran into both Daryl Parks and Ben Crump in the lobby of a San Francisco hotel and we discussed the case. We were all in

---

[1]The US Court of Appeals for the Eleventh Circuit hears appeals on cases from federal district courts in the states of Georgia, Florida, and Alabama prior to any such federal case being able to reach the United States Supreme Court.

shock at what happened. I also felt some hopelessness in that moment. Here we are in a nice hotel in San Francisco having come a long way from our chance meeting on a Tallahassee street in September 1995. We were all successful. We all had other prominent friends and colleagues. But in that moment, none of that mattered as we had just witnessed a grave injustice that we could not prevent despite our trappings of power. That night I thought about the advice or guidance we could give to young African-American men to help them navigate the feelings they must be experiencing right now. What could we say to help them to avoid dangerous situations like this?

While the Trayvon Martin case did not involve police violence, it did involve someone who failed in his pursuit of a career in law enforcement. George Zimmerman tried to operate in a quasi-security role by leading his local neighborhood watch association as he tried to mimic the bravado of a police officer. It is not clear to any of us how Trayvon could have avoided being followed, pursued, and ultimately killed by George Zimmerman. It occurred to each of us that the jury placed a certain value on George Zimmerman's life and presumed that his life warranted being defended. That jury, regrettably, did not give Trayvon Martin the same benefit of the doubt or the presumption that he, too, had a right to self-defense. After all, the only objective and incontrovertible evidence in the entire case was that George Zimmerman instigated the whole episode by following Trayvon Martin and disobeying a police order not to do so. That's the only evidence that has never been challenged. Even if Trayvon did punch George Zimmerman first, the jury had to presume that he did not have the right to fear for his own safety as he was followed by a stranger to warrant self-defense. More troubling is that perhaps that jury subconsciously felt that Trayvon's life did not have the same value as Zimmerman's life to justify an aggressive self-defense. Unfortunately, that episode while not police related is instructive to black boys and men on how a jury may perceive the value of their life without the benefit of having their voice represented. In light of this apparent lack of value attributed to lives of black men, we want to try to avoid escalation where possible and preserve your ability to be heard in a different setting, like in front of a judge or jury if it rises to that level. Admittedly, recent events suggest that you may not get the outcome you want in the judicial system, but you will learn ways to survive and come out on the other side alive. In hearing your side of the story this country will have to take a deep look inward to assess whether these judicial results truly reflect the values of the United States of America.

On July 17, 2014 in Staten Island, New York, Eric Garner was approached by police on a street corner and questioned about allegedly selling untaxed cigarettes. In his expression of frustration at what felt like police harassment to him, the 6'3" 340lbs Garner refused to comply with an order from a plainclothes police officer. That officer was later joined by other police officers who all confronted Garner about his activity and his refusal to obey a police order. Garner was tackled by three to four police officers, taken to the ground, and placed in an illegal choke hold.[2] In addition to having a rear choke hold on his neck, a police officer drove his knee in to Garner's mid spine area as he pled with officers that he could not breathe and repeated that cry for help eleven times. Garner died at the scene and his death was ruled a homicide. Even though Garner's death was ruled a homicide by a medical examiner, a New York grand jury refused to indict the police officer who was videotaped using a choke hold that NYPD has banned. Since this incident was captured on videotape for all to witness, the grand jury decision really struck a nerve with most of the American public. Not to excuse the police officers in this case of their responsibility, but the fact remains that Garner initially resisted the police when they attempted to take him into custody, which goes against one of the core principles we discuss later in our book.

Black men have died or been harmed during encounters with police when certain assumptions were

---

[2] Most US police departments ban the use of rear choke holds or in Mix Martial Arts a hold known as a "rear naked choke" given its near certainty to cause severe bodily harm and potentially death. New York City banned this type of choke hold in 1993.

made about them and their propensity to be engaged in criminal activity. The following tragic encounters seem to be rooted more in an irrational fear on the police officers' part rather than in reality. In September 2014, South Carolina state trooper Sean Groubert pulled over Levar Jones for a traffic violation. Trooper Groubert asked Mr. Jones to show his driver's license and Mr. Jones complied with the request by reaching into his vehicle to retrieve his license. As he was doing this, Trooper Groubert shot Mr. Jones several times for no apparent reason. Twelve-year old Tamir Rice of Cleveland, Ohio was playing with a toy gun in a park near his home like countless other American boys have done. He was shot dead within two seconds of police arriving on the scene following a 911 call in which the caller said a person is pointing what appears to be a toy gun. In February 1999, unarmed Amadou Diallo was shot at 41 times by four plainclothes police officers and struck 19 times. The officers alleged that Diallo fit the description of a rape suspect. These officers were not in uniform so Diallo likely was startled to be approached by four unfamiliar men in an aggressive manner. Diallo reached to grab his wallet and was fired at 41 times and killed.

Twenty-four year old Jonathan Ferrell, a former Florida A&M football player, was in an early morning car accident on September 14, 2013 in the Charlotte, North Carolina area. Likely dazed and disoriented from the accident, Ferrell sought help at a nearby home and startled the homeowner prompting her to call the police. When police arrived on the scene Ferrell ran towards them seeking help. Charlotte-Mecklenburg police officer Randall Kerrick fatally shot Ferrell several times. Finally, another inexplicable killing of a young black man occurred in August 2014 when 22 year-old John Crawford was gunned down by two Beavercreek, Ohio police officers as he was shopping in a Walmart store because he was carrying an unboxed toy assault rifle. Video surveillance footage showed John Crawford holding the toy gun in an unthreatening manner inside the store as he also talked on his cell phone. Ronald Ritchie placed a blatantly misleading 911 call stating that John Crawford was waving the gun and threatening other customers. Beavercreek Police officers Sergeant Darkow and Officer Williams arrived on the scene with their own assault rifles and opened fire on Crawford killing him. As in the Trayvon Martin case and Michael Brown case in Ferguson, another friend of mine was the lawyer for the family of John Crawford. My college classmate and friend of 25 years Dayton, Ohio attorney Michael Wright represented the Crawford family and shared quite a few insights on the case with me. Given my proximity to these three nationally talked about tragedies, I along with my co-author feel compelled to offer our insights on how to prevent the next death given our own personal experiences in these types of circumstances.

Adrian and I have had numerous conversations discussing all of these events. I could tell that these events frustrated him because he knows that most police officers are good people who are not trying to hurt citizens, but to protect them. Adrian has said, "Eric, these few bad apples make us all look bad." He has also been upset by some of the police conduct that he felt could have been changed to preserve life. I could tell he was torn, however, because of the difficulties he has personally experienced as a police officer in dealing with the public. I recall Adrian calling me one day telling me how he had to fight this guy who we both knew as he was trying to make an arrest. Over the years, I have heard numerous stories from Adrian about being spit at, punched and cursed out. These stories seemed unbelievable to me because Adrian is such a good-natured person. I could not see how someone could treat him that way. I am convinced that Adrian is a man without a single mean bone in his body. Given that we were friends from the age of 10, I have had the occasion to observe him in many different settings and circumstances and I can honestly say that I have never seen him conduct himself violently or aggressively toward another person. Notwithstanding his demeanor and nature, citizens have tried to hurt him and resist his authority when he is serving them through police work.

I reminded Adrian with gratitude about the pointers he gave me for interacting with police if I was pulled over for a traffic infraction. When Adrian provided me guidance on how to respond to police he allowed me to step into their world and to understand what they are concerned with during traffic stops or any other encounter. It is important to remember that they are investigating a crime or traffic violation. Adrian made it clear to me that police officers approach traffic stops or any other investigative situation with extreme caution and high alert. Hearing Adrian's perspective and understanding police mindset of heightened alertness and caution has helped me appreciate the importance of conducting myself in a manner that would help put a police officer at ease. Particularly because I know that I pose no threat to them, I approach them as such with no intention or perception of threat. Adrian made it clear to me that the police officer at the time of the encounter does not know that I am not a threat. We have discussed how that mindset on my part and my empathic behavior has led to uneventful encounters. Adrian and I decided that if we shared some of what we have both learned over the years being on both sides of the equation as an attorney and a policeman we could help reduce the number of hostile incidents between police and black men. Unfortunately, these recent tragedies make for only a handful of violent encounters that police have had with African-American men and boys. Many police departments have not or do not accurately report to the federal government deaths following encounters with police so many other violent and tragic encounters likely exist that have never been reported or acknowledged.

Many of us remember the March 3, 1991 police beating of Rodney King in Los Angeles that later sparked the LA riots that caused 53 deaths, 2000 injuries, and nearly $1 billion dollars in property damage and loss. Some of these well-known stories and some that are not as widely publicized engender a sense of hopelessness among black parents trying to figure out what to tell their young black boys about encounters with the police. Wives, sisters, mothers, fathers, grandparents, aunts, uncles, other relatives and friends have a genuine and very real fear of whether or not an African-American male in their lives will survive an encounter with the police. Adrian and I wanted to strike a balance between the legitimate fears, frustrations, and concerns of African-American men and boys while also providing a perspective on police officers and the many competing feelings, fears, and duties that they have to manage as they do their work on the public's behalf. This book seeks to increase the odds of survival following encounters with police. In addition, this book seeks to provide an alternative outlet for expressing the understandable frustrations and anger experienced by black men and boys when they encounter bad police. While we recognize that deeper issues of racial prejudice and systemic racism play into the deadly encounters with police, we are more focused on educating black men and boys on strategies and tactics to de-escalate tension during an encounter.

CHAPTER 2:
MISTRUST BETWEEN
AFRICAN-AMERICAN MEN AND POLICE

Adrian and I personally know about 35 black men who have been murdered from our small community. We both have a host of childhood friends and acquaintances in the prison system. Let's compare some age range statistics that show an alarming increase in incarceration rates over the years: 69% of black men who were high school dropouts born between 1975-1979 have spent time in prison[3] while nearly 42% percent of black men born between 1960-1964 have spent time in prison.[4] As Malcolm Gladwell pointed out in his book *David and Goliath, Underdogs, Misfits, and The Art of Battling Giants,* each of these prisoners has a black father, brother, cousin, nephew, uncle or other relative who has also experienced the ill effects of the penal system through the eyes of their black male relative.[5]

---

[3]Malcolm Gladwell, *David and Goliath, Underdogs, Misfits and the Art of Battling Giants,* (2013), *214*
[4]Ibid.
[5]Ibid.

Gladwell aptly points out that police in the eyes of those with such an affiliation are often viewed as the enemy.[6] This high concentration of African-Americans being incarcerated or otherwise under the penal system oversight fosters an "us versus them" mindset. It is difficult to empathize with or humanize others when we view them through the lens of oppressor versus the oppressed.

In addition to the fact that a high percentage of younger African-Americans have such a contentious relationship with law enforcement, African-American men have a long history of encounters with police that have resulted in maiming, abuse and death that makes it difficult to view police in a favorable light. In light of the recent events of Ferguson, Missouri; Beavercreek, Ohio; and Staten Island, New York, civil rights organizations, government agencies, politicians, social organizations and others are launching programs and initiatives to help bridge this seemingly great divide between law enforcement and

---

[6] Ibid.

the African-American community.[7]

One example of an initiative aimed at addressing some of the more entrenched social issues is President Obama's creation of the Task Force on 21st Century Policing to further understand some of the underlying causes that foster mistrust among police and minority communities.[8] We recognize the importance of these initiatives that must take place to address problems of mistrust and we are hopeful that dialogue and protest lead to concrete changes in the way police interact with the black community and to changes in the way the black community views the police and interacts with them. We are not going to delve too deeply into those institutional changes that we agree need to be made and the relational changes that also need to occur through authentic

---

[7] Missouri Governor Jay Nixon created the Ferguson Commission made up of local lawyers, business leaders, current and former police officers, pastors and even a protestor to address lingering relationship problems between the police and community. *Nixon Announces Members of Ferguson Commission,*St. Louis Post Dispatch, November 19, 2014. Similarly, Ohio Governor John Kasich impaneled a task force to improve relationships between police and communities. *Task Force Created in Wake of Police Action,Wall Street JournalWeekend Edition,* December 6-7, 2014, A5.

[8] *Task Force's Chief Familiar to Many in Washington,* Washington Post, December 5, 2014 A5.

dialogue. Those changes will only come through a sustained effort and commitment on the part of police departments, community organizations, government involvement, and members of the most affected communities staying engaged with each other and implementing recommendations that come out of sustained and engaged dialogue. In writing this book, we are not ignorant to the deep mistrust nor do we discount the real grievances that exist regarding interactions with police. Our focus, however, is more short-term in that we are focusing this dialogue on the immediate instance of an encounter with police. We address what to do in that moment and suggest approaches to minimize the chance of conflict. We appreciate the pain and the resentment that may rise naturally in thinking about the deaths of black men and women at the hands of police. We appreciate why that history and background may make some of our suggestions difficult to accept. We are committed to one thing: we want you to make it home safely after an encounter with police.

CHAPTER 3:
POLICE OFFICERS ARE HUMAN BEINGS

Before we get into the very simple, but admittedly not easily done, practical steps to survive a police encounter, we need to spend a moment to talk about police. The first thing that we want to stress to every reader is that police officers are human beings. We recognize that systemic failures in training and lack of diversity in many departments along with pockets of corruption makes it difficult for some black men to view police officers as human beings.[9] Your anger or resentment may cloud your view of that person in uniform standing on the other side of you during a traffic stop or during a brief detention for questioning. When you think of "protect and serve" you are probably not expecting a military style vehicle rolling down the streets like we witnessed in Ferguson, Missouri. Notwithstanding those failures by some police

---

[9] Twelve year old Tamir Rice was shot and killed by a police officer that one Ohio police department deemed unfit to serve and there were reports of this police officer possibly being emotionally unstable as he would cry at the gun range. This police officer was still able to get a job with the Cleveland Police Department so this is an example of a likely system failure.

departments and your negative feelings towards police— justified or not—police officers have feelings such as fear, anger, embarrassment, hopelessness, despair, frustration, joy, happiness, love, empathy, sympathy and every other feeling that each of us has. When we encounter police in their well-pressed uniforms and official demeanor, we somehow lose sight of the fact that the police officer is a human being just like us. Moreover, the police officer wants to leave the encounter with you alive just as much as you would like to leave the encounter with him alive and like you, he or she wants no unnecessary tension or escalation.

The reason for the stop or the encounter is more likely than not going to be a point of disagreement between you and the police. Were you actually speeding? Do you really resemble a robbery suspect? What was it about you that made you look suspicious? You should take some comfort in the fact that the police officer cannot ultimately find you guilty of anything. Your guilt or innocence has to be determined in a court of law. Therefore, you should politely and calmly state your case to the police officer briefly, and not waste your time arguing with them on the scene. A prosecutor, judge or jury will ultimately decide whether they believe you or the police officer. Remind yourself that the police officer has an important role in the judicial process, but that role is not one of the final decision-maker. If you escalate an encounter with police to a point where violence occurs or your death, then only the police officer's story will be told. A judge, jurors or prosecutors would be forced to speculate on what your story or version of events was. Given conscious and unconscious bias in our society a favorable presumption is not likely to be given to your side of the story especially if you are no longer alive to tell it.

Adrian and I will discuss this very important point in more detail later because the mindset you take into encounters with police is very important and may in fact determine how you will leave them. Knowing that your ultimate goal is to get home safely, think about the police encounter as a temporary event and only a small part of a much larger process that you have a right to in order to receive justice. We recognize that there may be costs to you in this process as lawyers cost money and you may need a lawyer to help you in the process. A court may appoint you an attorney or you may seek assistance from an organization like the National Bar Association.[10] It is possible that you may not even need to hire a lawyer as other non-judicial avenues exist for you to challenge police misconduct. We can appreciate the fear or apprehension that African-American men and boys may have about getting entangled in the legal system. It can be scary. The irony with this fear, however, is that you may be forced into this system either way by bad police officers who others before you failed to confront using the legal system or an administrative process. By taking a stand through the proper forum and following through, you literally start to build a web or shield of protection around yourself as well as other black men who may otherwise encounter rogue police.

---

[10] The National Bar Association is the largest and oldest network of predominately African-American attorneys who are very active in fighting for the rights of minorities.

Practical Step Number 1 for Surviving an Encounter with Police: Remember that Police Officers are Human Beings

If you are being pulled over for a traffic violation or stopped on the street and questioned by a police officer, keep this following point in mind before you say or do anything: the police officer is a human being just like you and the police officer has a job to do. When Adrian and I discussed his own decision to become a police officer, Adrian expressed sincere altruistic motives for joining the force. Adrian told me that he did not like to see people get bullied. He also believed that he could serve others and help others in need or in crisis which is consistent with his Christian faith. Adrian says that he was not made for a desk job and that the mobility of police work was intriguing to him. Above all, Adrian made it clear that he actually gets major satisfaction from protecting others and serving them which is the motto of police work. Adrian gets to do a job that fits with his personality trait of wanting to help others.

POLICE OFFICERS HAVE A JOB TO DO

Police officers are charged with keeping order in the public. Police officers are responsible for trying to keep burglars out of your home and keeping you safe from violent criminals, who might want to cause you bodily harm, steal your bike or car, or hurt one of your family members. Police officers are also responsible for making sure that traffic laws are obeyed so that small children do not get run over by reckless speeding drivers or that your parents are not rear-ended and paralyzed by some speeding driver who runs a red light and plows into the back of their car. Police officers have to deal with tragic incidents like this almost daily so you might consider how you would feel if you witnessed the aftermath of speeding drivers running over a family dog, damaging a parked car, or killing a small child. Those experiences just might give you a little bit of an edge when you pull someone over for speeding. If you put yourself in the police officer's shoes, you may see how it might be difficult to separate feelings related to arresting the speeding driver who killed the

6-year old girl, and the officer's attitude towards you for driving 48 mph in a 25 mph speed zone. That police officer for very good reason may have a slight edge or attitude with you for your speeding. The officer may have witnessed first-hand the pain caused by such behavior. Remember that same police officer may have witnessed parents falling to their knees in agony at the sight of their dead child who was run over by a speeding driver. Police officers all too often experience the worst side of humanity. They are human beings and deserve to be cut a little slack for not being happy when they witness conduct from you which may produce horrific results they've observed in other circumstances. Always remember that police officers are human beings and they are deeply impacted by what they see on the job daily.

POLICE OFFICER'S WORK BENEFITS YOU

In addition to remembering that police officers have a job to do, take a brief moment to consider the benefits of police work to you. In short, we have peace and stability by and large because we have police officers who keep the peace. We will address the bad police officers who themselves break the law and undermine peace. The vast majority of police officers, however, are doing their jobs correctly and their work benefits you. If someone steals your car, you call the police and hope that they retrieve it. If someone steals your bike, you can file a police report and have a chance at having your property returned. If someone assaults a member of your family, it will be a police officer who ultimately arrests that person and removes them from the streets where they could continue to hurt your family members and others.

Police officers maintain safety. When police officers ticket speeding drivers, it reduces the chances of one of your family members being hit by a speeding car. When police officers ticket someone for aggressive driving, it makes it less likely that you will get rear-ended and end up with permanent damage to your spine. These benefits may seem vague or of little to no consequence from where you stand, but they are real benefits. When you encounter the police, remember that their job benefits you, personally. Even if you disagree vehemently that you resemble the robbery suspect, police vigilance around finding that suspect will make it less likely that the suspect eventually robs you. We are asking you to make a slight shift in mindset when you encounter the police. Please remember that police officers are human. Remember that they are just doing their jobs with imperfect information. Finally, please remember that the role of proper policing has a direct and tangible benefit to you. Please try to keep these things in mind when you encounter police.

AS HUMAN BEINGS, POLICE OFFICERS MAKE MISTAKES

Alexander Pope wrote "to err is human; to forgive, divine."[11] Police officers are no different than you or me in that regard and, therefore, they are going to make mistakes. If you are stopped by a police officer because you fit the profile of a burglary suspect, just remember

---

[11] Alexander Pope, *An Essay on Criticism*

that the police officer is a human being with limited information. The police officer may not know exactly what the person looks like. Even when the police have a photo of a suspect, they still have to make their best guess whether a particular person fits that profile. While we would like for them to get it right 100% of the time, that expectation is unrealistic and unfair. How many of you have achieved a perfect score on every test you have taken in school? How many of you have performed your job perfectly without making any mistakes at all? Do you think you should be yelled at or called curse words for your mistakes? If not, then why would you think it is fair for police officers to be yelled at or called abusive names for their mistakes?

In a democracy like ours in the United States, there are certain costs to the freedoms we enjoy. Your reaction to being questioned or interrogated by police due to mistaken identity can totally de-escalate the encounter if you just take some simple steps that we'll discuss shortly. But first and foremost just remember that the police officer stopping you is human and is subject to making errors. The majority of police officers are neither bad nor mean spirited. Some are and we will discuss how to deal with them as well. In all circumstances when you encounter police officers keep their humanity first and foremost in mind, as this will definitely help you to lower, if not eliminate the risk that may come with any unnecessary escalation. Below is a chart of police commands or requests in the context of an encounter and words or actions that are likely to escalate and words or actions to de-escalate any tension during an encounter.

Police Officer Statement/ Action	Words/Actions that Escalate	Words/Actions to De-escalate
"Driver's license & registration please!"	What the f_ _ _ did I do? Why the hell you pull me over?	"Hi Officer, I am going to reach in my back pocket for my driver's license and then my glove box for my registration. Is that Ok Officer?"

"You know you ran a stop sign back there?"	"No I didn't, there ain't no stop sign back there!"	"Officer if I did, I did not do it intentionally."
"You know you were traveling 50 mph in a 35!"	"I was not speeding! Y'all always harassing me!"	"Officer, I make no excuses for speeding. My license is in my back pocket may I reach for it?" Do not argue or raise your voice.
"You fit the description of a robbery suspect" while holding their gun	Sudden move. "Hell no I don't look like no suspect! You just profiling me you racist cop!"	Hands visible and no sudden move. "Officer I am sure once you see my ID you will realize that I am not that suspect. May I retrieve my license please?" Move slowly and deliberately the whole time

"Freeze don't move!"	Sudden move. "What the f_ _ _ is going on? Why you messing with me?"	Don't move & don't speak until asked a question. Answer slowly "Sir, I was on my way home from school. I have my student ID to prove who I am officer." Respectful tone and do not argue.
"Get over here"	"What bitch?" -- Punch police	"Yes sir. Did I do something wrong officer? I have my ID officer. I'd like to contact a lawyer sir"
Police officer grabs you	Resist and fight back	Do not resist ever. "Officer I will not resist you. I'll comply with what you want me to do. I'd like to contact a lawyer."

Officer points gun at you	Run or try to fight	Never Run. Never Resist. Put your hands up and follow the officer's instructions. After things are calm ask to speak with an attorney. Police asserted that both Eric Garner and Michael Brown put up some type of resistance. Please do not resist.

POLICE OFFICERS SEE THE WORST SIDE OF HUMANITY DAILY

We believe that having empathy for police officers will go a long way towards you surviving an encounter with police. Imagine having to spend 8 to 12 hours per day witnessing the most horrendous conduct known to humanity and cleaning up the aftermath of such misconduct. Police officers respond to calls related to domestic violence. They see a spouse battered and beaten beyond recognition. Police officers have to encounter and rescue children with broken arms and legs from abusive parents. They see children mutilated from cigarette burns. Police officers are there to move bullet ridden dead bodies after a violent gang confrontation. They retrieve decomposed bodies of missing college students and have to live with the memory of the horrid stench of a decomposed corpse. Police officers do all this work hoping to make it home to see their children and families.

Police officers put their lives at risk on every call.

Imagine the stress you would be under if every time you performed your job duties, you knew you might end up dead. What if you had a gun drawn on you or have someone you are trying to protect curse and spit at you? These are everyday occurrences for police officers and they often do this for pay that is too low when you consider the risk to their lives daily and the inordinate level of stress they must endure. Just remember that the cop who pulls you over may have, just hours prior, removed the dead body of a young girl from an abandoned building. He might have had an abusive husband try to fight him as he tried to remove him from the family home. She or he may have been chasing a burglar who sped away from the scene of the crime at high speed. In short, we are asking that when you encounter a police officer, just take a few seconds to think about what they have encountered that day and see if you can avoid adding any unnecessary tension to their lives by being rude or disrespectful towards them. If a police officer is rude and disrespectful to you first, we will tell you how to more forcefully deal with them. Yelling or getting into an argument with them will accomplish nothing and likely put you at risk. Recognizing that a fair amount of distrust exists between police and the African-American community, each side taking a step back to be empathetic and mindful of the other's humanity will go a long way towards reducing tensions.

POLICE OFFICERS GET KILLED IN THE LINE OF DUTY

When you encounter a police officer either in a traffic context or a non-traffic stop situation, remember that every officer you encounter is keenly aware that another police officer was killed during a similar event. You should know that police officers review training videos of other police officers who have been murdered during a routine traffic stop or police officers being shot and killed while responding to a domestic disturbance call in a family home. Imagine for a moment that you walked into your school or your job and you were reminded that during the course of your routine someone may pull out a gun and shoot you in the head or pull out a knife and slit your throat. Bear in mind that police officers like our soldiers returning from war may also suffer from Post-traumatic stress disorder (PTSD) and their heightened sense of alertness, formality, and seriousness may be a by-product of high stress police work.

Every single time a police officer has an encounter with anyone of any ethnic background or gender, it may be the last thing they do. Certainly the weight of such worry commands that we as African-American men take that mindset into consideration whenever we encounter a police officer. The police officer's edge may have more to do with the training video he just viewed in which another officer somewhere in the US was murdered as he was pulling someone over for speeding. Many police cruisers have dash cams that record traffic stops and other encounters that occur around the police cruiser. These dash cams have been useful for both confirming and denying police misconduct. The dash cams also chronicle just how dangerous the job of policing can be.

From 2000 - 2014, over two thousand police officers died in the line of duty.[12] Not all of these officers were killed by a criminal directly, but may have died due to an accident during a high speed chase or in performing other job duties. These police officers had mothers, fathers, husbands, wives, children, siblings and friends whom they also left behind heartbroken. They also left behind fellow police officers with a stark reminder of just how dangerous their jobs can be. As African-American men, we are just asking African-American men and all others who encounter police to simply consider these facts and how these facts may impact how police officers interact with the public. Admittedly, when you are pulled over or stopped as you walk down the street to be questioned, a rush of adrenaline will no doubt course through your veins. Please try to take a deep breath before you do or say anything and remember this police officer is only trying to do his or her job, even if they are ultimately proven wrong about charging you with an offense. If they are not doing their job and doing something more sinister, we outline in

---

[12] See Officer Down Memorial Page at http://www.odmp.org

detail how you can make them pay for their bad behavior. *Always remember you cannot make a police officer pay for their misconduct at the time that it happens.*

The police officer actually does not know at the time of the encounter whether you are a real suspect or not. The police officer may have a defective laser or radar gun that inaccurately clocked your speed. In any case, the police officer's role in our system is to make their best professional guess or judgment based upon their training, prior experience, and appropriate evidence. A prosecutor, judge, or jury will make the final decision about whether those actions were right or wrong. In fact, your positive demeanor during the encounter may even change that police officer's mind about why they stopped you. I actually had this happen to me and will discuss this in the book. In all of these cases, just remember that the police officer is a human being. The police officer has either personally experienced the loss of a fellow police officer in their city, county or state or has been made aware of another police officer's demise in another part of the country.

Operating under a threat of potential death may make police officers appear unfriendly or even hostile, but your own attitude and conduct can alter this mood.

KINDNESS AND RESPECT GO A LONG WAY WITH THE VAST MAJORITY OF POLICE OFFICERS

Everyone likes to be treated with respect and dignity. Police officers are no different in that regard. In fact, given the risks they take daily to protect the public, showing them a little respect in either a traffic encounter or a non-traffic stop is not too much to ask. One of the biggest reasons I attribute to having nearly no issues or escalation with any officer who has pulled me over for speeding, vehicle defect or another traffic infraction is that I always spoke in a calm and respectful tone. I also tried to empathize with the officer stopping me. I referred to the police officer as "sir" or "ma'am" or as "Officer." I never raised my voice with them and I never contorted my face as if to express surprise or anger at the idea of them stopping me. I have been stopped about 14 to 16 times for traffic infractions or vehicle defects with my car and I have only received four tickets—that's right only four. In almost all instances, I received a stern warning and interestingly enough a look of gratitude that I treated them with dignity and respect. I honestly think that the police officers who pulled me over may have had their own preconceived notions of how I would react and were likely relieved that I never argued or even tried to get out of the tickets for that matter. In two instances, the police officers received more urgent calls which required them to leave and I do believe I would have received a ticket in at least one of those instances. We all have an inclination at times to resist authority. We may disobey an order from our parents or not pay attention to instructions from a teacher. It is not uncommon to have feelings of rebellion at times, but those feelings need to be checked when encountering police. The stakes are too high to let pride, ego, or selfishness dictate that things have to go your way in that moment. If you did something wrong like speeding, then you have to pay. If you did not do anything wrong and the police officer is making a mistake, you are not going to win that argument on the spot so save it for another day after you have made it home safely.

This is not a book that will help you to get out of a traffic ticket. This is a book to help you to avoid the fate of Michael Brown, Eric Garner, or Levar Jones. This book is about getting you home safely after an encounter with police. For the sake of your family and for yourself, simply be polite when encountering police. Even if the police officer is rude to you just consider that a day or two ago, that officer may have had to pick up the body of a child run over by a speeding driver. Show the officer some empathy. Show them some respect. Be kind, respectful and calm and you will get home safely and they will get home safe as well.

Later in this book, I discuss a couple of encounters that I have had and provide clear guidelines about what to do in traffic stop situations. I recall a traffic encounter I had with a police officer that had a totally unexpected and positive outcome for me. I believe that this surprising

outcome stemmed from me being intentional and conscious about acknowledging the police officer's humanity and feelings. Instead of physical or verbal conflict, this police officer and I shared a genuine moment of connection. About a year after the 9/11 terrorists attacks, I was doing my routine commute home from America Online, Inc.'s headquarters in Dulles, Virginia where I served as a corporate lawyer to my home in Washington, DC. Washington area drivers are familiar with a shortcut travelers take through the Pentagon— as in the headquarter for the mightiest military in the world—to reach Interstate 395 which runs into DC if you are coming from Interstate 66 which traverses northern Virginia. I took this route daily for years when I worked at AOL. This particular day had been a horrible day at work as I was negotiating a complex deal for AOL with one of the professional sports leagues and the negotiations were brutal. In addition to the protracted legal negotiations that day, I had a few personal things blow up on me that day. It was one of those days where everything that could go wrong went wrong. As I was making my way through the Pentagon parking lot I was traveling at a high speed because I just needed to get home and relax. All of a sudden, lights flared behind me, just as I was getting ready to get onto I-395 to make my way into DC. I pulled over to the side of the road and turned on my interior lights, as it was dark outside. I placed both of my hands on the steering wheel and waited for the officer who was very cautiously approaching my vehicle.

"Do you know why I am pulling you over?" the police officer asked. "Officer, I am not sure but I suspect that I was speeding." I said matter-of-factly. "Yes, you were. You were going 48 mph in a 35 mph zone," he said. The Pentagon was on heightened alert during this time. Things were always a little edgy going through the Pentagon. "Sir, I am going to reach in my back pocket to get my license. Is that Ok?" I asked humbly. He said, "Sure and get me your registration and insurance information as well." I replied, "Officer I need to reach in my glove box to get those for you. Is that OK?" He answered, "Yes." During this time, I was focused on making him feel at ease because I knew he had to be on the hunt for potential terrorists. After all, the Pentagon was clearly a target of terrorists as it was attacked on 9/11 about 200 yards from where we were parked. After finding my documents, as I was getting ready to hand them to the officer, I looked him in the eyes and I think he could see that something was really bothering me that had nothing to do with his stopping me or with any criminal suspicion. He did not get anger from me. He did not get resistance from me. He got an authentic view of where I was as a human in that moment—down in the dumps about something. As I looked at him, I said in a low voice "Officer, have you ever had one of those days?" The officer looked down at my driver's license and while tapping it on my insurance card and registration card he looked back at me directly in the eye with a look of understanding. He paused and exclaimed "Hell yes I have!" As he slowly reached back to hand me my license, insurance card, and registration without even checking me out or running my information through his system, he added "Slow down when you are driving through here sir and have a better night."

The only thing that I could attribute that outcome to was a moment where two guys—human beings--who happened to meet in the context of a police traffic stop connected. Without expecting to get anything from that police officer that evening except for a prompt dismissal after receiving a ticket, I was intentional about giving him respect and about making sure he did not feel or perceive any threat from me. I figured this guy is on the lookout for Al Qaeda so he sure as heck doesn't need some disgruntled lawyer making his job any harder. I also connected with him on a human level without any expectation for what that genuine moment might bring. I believe that my deliberate actions around retrieving items allowed him to see me as a human who was also showing concern for his safety. Through our exchange of mutual respect based upon each of us acknowledging the other's humanity, I not only avoided being given a speeding ticket, but was given something much greater than that. That officer gave me the gift of empathy just as I had given it to him. In that moment the police officer felt my pain and decided not to add to it. This is not a road map for how to get out of a ticket, but a true story about what is possible when we can be present with each other in a moment without telling ourselves a story about how the other person "is" or what the other person "always does" in a situation like this. In that moment of mutual acknowledgment of humanity and exchanging respect, I passed through one of the most fortified facilities in the world after violating traffic laws without so much as having my driver's license or license plate checked out.

CHAPTER 4:
BAD POLICE EXIST AND THEY CAN BE PUNISHED

PRACTICAL STEP NUMBER 2 FOR SURVIVING ENCOUNTERS WITH POLICE: BAD POLICE OFFICERS CAN BE PUNISHED, BUT NOT ON THE SPOT AND NOT BY YOU

When you do encounter an abusive police officer or a bully with a badge, do not respond in the moment. Just remember to **comply now and contest later**. Take a deep breath and remember that you have several options to have the abusive police officer punished. Your only objective during the encounter is to leave it peacefully and unharmed. Most people think that if a police officer verbally abuses them or otherwise treats them inappropriately, they have to just take it and that they have no recourse. That is simply not true. Alternatively, some people believe that their only recourse against abusive officers is to argue with them; insult them; or try to get them to change their mind about what happened. This is not the right approach, and you are always going to lose if you choose any of those responses.

You actually have a number of potential avenues to redress any wrongs committed against you that are much more powerful than you getting into a tit for tat argument with a police officer at the scene. Just remember you are never going to win an argument with a police officer, but you might win an argument before a judge or jury. You also might win an argument before that police officer's Commanding Officer or Supervisor. Never forget that if the confrontation escalates physically, the police officer has a gun and other weapons to injure you. You should, therefore, not physically resist a police officer and make it clear that you will comply with all orders and instructions. Remember, if you resist physically or you run and the officer uses deadly force on you, your story will never be heard. It's rare to have video footage and even with eyewitness accounts it is difficult to get a clear picture of what actually happened if you cannot present your story.

Consider how many different versions of events were presented from eyewitness testimony during the grand jury's investigation of Darren Wilson for killing Michael Brown in Ferguson, Missouri. The competing versions of what actually happened raised more questions than provided answers. Only two people really know what happened and one of them is dead. **Comply now and contest later.**

File a Complaint against an Abusive Officer at the Local Police Station

If you encounter an abusive police officer, being unprofessional towards you, you can simply ask for the officer's name and badge number during the stop. If you feel that by asking for that information you may escalate the situation, try to note the vehicle number on the officer's police cruiser. Additionally, the officer's name should be on any ticket you receive. You have the right to go to that officer's precinct or to the local police headquarter to file a formal written complaint against the police officer. By filing a formal written complaint you get a chance to air your grievance in the appropriate forum and by taking this formal action you can get much more satisfaction than you get from insulting the officer or engaging in a futile argument because your formal complaint ensures the following:

- The police officer will be investigated for their conduct

- There is a record of the police officer's alleged misconduct

- This record may make the police officer think twice before abusing someone else

- Your report helps the next victim of that officer by making their accusation more believable

- If multiple complaints are filed, then the officer is more likely to be disciplined

- The police officer could be terminated if multiple allegations are on record

Make certain that you follow through to find out what the disposition of your written complaint is. This ensures you that a record was created in the police officer's employee file. You may find a supervisor who wants to talk with you about what the police officer did and that conversation may be an attempt to dissuade you from filing the written complaint. Make sure that you file your written complaint before you leave the station. Your written complaint on file establishes a record. The records may reveal a pattern of abuse and misconduct which makes it much more difficult for prosecutors or grand juries to dismiss additional complaints.

Contact an Elected Official to Complain about an Abusive Officer

You can always contact an elected official such as the mayor or county commissioner in the city or county where the police department is located. It is a part of local elected officials' responsibility to provide oversight of policing practices. If a number of citizens make their elected officials aware of alleged police misconduct, then those officials will be forced to act since no politician wants a paper trail of their neglect of duty. Moreover, you help to establish a paper trail with documentation of police misconduct and no action was taken. Complaints to the local police department about its abusive officers coupled with complaints to local elected officials can increase the likelihood of success if a lawsuit is subsequently filed by another victim of police misconduct.

Depending upon where the police department is located, there may be dedicated offices set up to receive citizen complaints about police misconduct or potential civil rights violations. You can conduct a simple web search to find out what other resources may be available in the jurisdiction where you encountered the police or visit www.survivethepolice.com.

Contact the United States Department of Justice

You can notify the United States Department of Justice (DOJ) if you feel you were being racially profiled. In recent years the DOJ has been investigating racial profiling incidents involving minority drivers. The DOJ also keeps statistics on police activity which is why it is important for you to take the time to file a formal written complaint with the local police department and notify the DOJ if the incident is egregious enough (e.g., police officer calls you a racial epithet). The DOJ can also investigate a local police department, appoint an independent monitor over the police department or take other legal remedial measures.

File a Civil Rights Lawsuit

In egregious cases of police misconduct or abuse, you may have a claim under Section 1983 of the Civil Rights Act. Section 1983 provides a way for citizens to be compensated monetarily when a government official does something improper that violates your constitutional rights. We'll broadly refer to this as a civil rights violation which gives you the right to file a civil rights suit. A civil rights suit is certainly appropriate in egregious cases like the Rodney King beating and we will likely see civil rights suits filed against the officers in some of the other cases we highlighted at the outset of the book.

Congress enacted this law—Section 1983--in order to protect the rights guaranteed to all Americans by the 14th Amendment. Under Section 1983, a victim of police abuse can file a lawsuit in federal court for police brutality. Police brutality may include:

- Excessive force
- Use of racial slur
- Lethal force

Some of your constitutional rights that can be violated by police and are frequent subjects of Section 1983 suits include:

- **Fourth Amendment:** A police officer touching your physical person (even with a baton or bullets) is a "seizure" under the Fourth Amendment. A police officer using a Taser on you may also violate this right.

- **Fifth Amendment:** If a police officer detains you and begins to interrogate you without reading your Miranda rights that interrogation may violate your Fifth Amendment right against self-incrimination. If detained by police and before being questioned, you have the right:
    - -To remain silent
    - -To have an attorney
    - -To be informed that your statements may be used against you

- **Fourteenth Amendment:** If a police officer utters a racial slur or some other form of verbal abuse based on your race, this conduct can violate your right to equal protection under the law.

The targets of a Section 1983 lawsuit can be:

City and county governments: Your lawsuit against a local police department would have to be a suit against the city in which the department operates instead of the police department itself. For example, the lawsuit would be known as John Doe versus The City of Chicago instead of the Chicago Police Department. This is also why it is important as citizens to report police misconduct to city and county government officials. Your filing of a formal written complaint against an abusive police officer creates a paper trail which may be helpful in the context of a future Section 1983 lawsuit. This information could be useful to a court to determine whether systemic problems exist with a police department.

The mayor of a city: You also have the option to sue the mayor of that city. This is also why it is important to not only file a formal written complaint of abusive policing at the local police station, but you should also send a letter to the mayor of the city or highest ranking government official. This creates a paper trail for future legal cases in the unfortunate event that your written complaint is not taken seriously by the authorities. Your complaint may result in an abusive police officer being disciplined. If, however, no action is taken against the police officer, there is at least a record that might help the next victim. Officials with supervisory authority over police departments who ignore citizen complaints (even if you are not a resident of the local jurisdiction) could possibly make it easier for the next victim of police misconduct to prevail in a lawsuit.

The police officer and their supervisor: In addition to suing the city and the mayor, you may also sue the police officer who abused you and their supervisor for any injuries or violations of your rights. Anytime anyone is in a lawsuit it is very stressful. Whatever stress you may experience during an encounter with the police would pale in comparison to the stress that a police officer will endure during a Section 1983 lawsuit for their abusive conduct. The results for the bad police officer can be severe as they can lose their job, have difficulty getting another job in law enforcement, and be publicly shamed for their prejudice or abuse of power.

Civil rights lawsuits are effective tools for righting obvious wrongs by police. It is worth pointing out that these lawsuits are not easily won. Police officers are entitled to what is known as "Qualified Immunity" which means that the law broadly protects police officers who perform their jobs as long as they do not use that official position to carry out misconduct that violates your civil rights. For example, a police officer cannot falsely accuse you of a crime and slap handcuffs on you simply because he is angry that you are dating his ex-girlfriend. If the purpose of the police officer's arrest of you was to punish you for dating his ex-girlfriend and not to enforce a law, then that officer is doing what our judicial system calls "acting under the color of law" while engaging in inappropriate conduct which violates your constitutional rights. As long as the police officer has probable cause to stop you or arrest you, they may avail themselves of Qualified Immunity which protects them from any liability. Police officers are entitled to use reasonable force to protect themselves without being subject to liability. If you pull a gun on a police officer, you are likely going to be shot and that officer is not likely to be found liable for shooting you. If you do not have a weapon and are not acting in a threatening manner in any other way, then any officer who shoots you could be punished both criminally and through a civil rights lawsuit. The goal of this book is to get you home safely so pay close attention to the steps we outline for you. Please set your ego or pride aside for the sake of getting you home safely. ***Comply now and contest later.*** You can reclaim your pride when you cause the police officer to be disciplined, fired, or forced to pay money damages to you. It is true that you may feel an intense amount of stress and humiliation in the moment the police officer violates your civil rights. You can put the bad police officer through the same amount or even more stress through a prolonged legal proceeding or simply by them knowing that their personnel file has documentation that will make it easier for them to be fired and more difficult for them to be promoted or find another job.

Earlier, we stated that you should file a complaint if you believe that a police officer acted abusively towards you. This would undoubtedly include a police officer using a racial slur against you. If you and others have previously filed written complaints with the local police department about the police officer's use of racist language, then that may make it easier to prove a case in court. Documenting the offending police officer's bad conduct may place that officer at greater risk of being found liable under Section 1983 for civil rights violations. Civil rights lawsuits under Section 1983 are complicated matters and we have resources for you at www.survivethepolice.com.

CHAPTER 5:
TRAFFIC ENCOUNTERS

PRACTICAL STEP NUMBER 3 FOR SURVIVING ENCOUNTERS WITH POLICE: IN TRAFFIC STOPS REMAIN CALM AND POLITE AND BE TRANSPARENT

In the fall of 2009, I was driving to my home in Northwest Washington, DC in the LeDroit Park neighborhood. I was in a business suit and it was approximately 8:30 PM. As I approached First Street, NW coming from one of Washington's main thoroughfare streets, New York Avenue, I was pulled over by what I thought was a single DC police cruiser. As I pulled over in my sports car, I was quickly surrounded by two other police cruisers. I quickly turned on the interior lights of the vehicle and placed both of my hands on the steering wheel so that the police officers could see my hands clearly. My immediate thought was that I was being racially profiled for driving a luxury car. As an African-American police officer approached my car very cautiously, he yelled "license and registration please!" I calmly asked "why am I being pulled over officer?" He replied, "The tint on your car window is too dark for DC regulations." I looked at him and said "Well officer I do not have any tint on my windows except what comes from the factory, but I am going to reach in the glove box to get my registration and insurance card if that is OK with you." He said, "Yes, it is and I need your license too!" I slowly reached into my glove box making deliberate moves all the way as another white male police officer was now standing in front of my car with his hand on his gun. I was puzzled as to why there were now four police cruisers surrounding my vehicle and a few officers surrounding me with hands on their guns.

Handing the officer my license, I said firmly back "Here are my driver's license and also my DC Bar License as I am an attorney and really want to understand why I am being surrounded for what sounds like a minor traffic violation." "I don't need your DC Bar license," the officer yelled back and tossed it back in the car." Although I was fearful for my life because some officers had their hands on their guns, I remained calm and resolved to seek retribution against all of these officers at another time and through another process other than arguing. I was angry, but I remained at ease because I knew that this was not the end of this encounter and they would have to answer for this overreaching conduct when I take legal action.

It was disheartening to me that this was happening to a successful African-American male driving in an expensive car in his own neighborhood. The African-American officer came back to my car after running my driver's license and tags, and said "Mr. Broyles, here is your driver's license and registration information back and I am not going to ticket you for this but get that tint checked out." I said, "Thank you Officer, but I will need your name and badge number along with every other police officer on this scene before we depart. I also need to know the name of your superior." The officer replied, "I'll give you that information but please come here and let me show you what I saw when I pulled up behind your vehicle," he spoke calmly—if not apologetically. As we walked back towards his cruiser, he pointed to my rear windshield. I said "Wow, I never noticed that but it does look like I have dark tint on the rear window. This is from the factory and I have never tinted the windows on any vehicle I own. I usually have the top down on this car and have never really noticed this." The police officer responded, "Yeah, DC does not allow for dark tint on vehicles and as you can see your rear windshield looks like it has dark tint from this angle."

I returned to my vehicle without getting any of the police officers' information, and I could understand why I was pulled over. What I could not understand and did not get an explanation for was why the excessive show of force and surrounding of my vehicle. I decided that I would pursue something with this, but wanted to reach out to the local precinct before calling then DC Mayor Adrian Fenty to complain. The next day, I called the local precinct and spoke with a person who actually handles citizen complaints against police officers. "Hi, I'd like to lodge a complaint against an officer and try to figure out why I was surrounded by police for an alleged violation of having tinted windows," I said. The representative from the police department asked me where this incident occurred. I said "On First Street near New York Avenue, Northwest." The lady then said, "Before you say anything else sir, can I ask you a question." "Sure," I replied. "Is your car silver and two-door?" She asked. I was astonished because I did not say my name or anything else about the stop. "Well, yes it is and how did you know to ask that?" I asked. She said, "Sir, we were looking for a murder suspect in that neighborhood who was reported to be fleeing the scene of the crime in a silver two-door coupe." A sigh of relief came over me as I just realized that I was not the victim of racial profiling as I had believed overnight. I heard myself reason the night before "Here I am a successful black man and I get pulled over for no valid reason except that I was driving while black." Then when the true and complete facts surfaced it turned out that there was indeed a valid reason for me being pulled over. In fact, as a resident of that neighborhood, I actually want the police to be diligent in searches for murder suspects within a mile of my home. I said, "Wow, thank you ma'am for letting me know this. I think this answers my questions and I wish the officers would have shared that with me." I did not file a written complaint.

This encounter was informative for a number of reasons. First, my perception of what was occurring during the traffic stop was totally different from the perspective of the police officers who surrounded me. On the one hand, I was simply returning to my home from a long day's work and had done nothing wrong. I thought that I was being racially profiled as I was a black man in an expensive car in a neighborhood that was in the process of rapid improvement but still had some pockets of high criminal activity. I was not speeding as I had just pulled off from a stop light at the time I saw the police lights behind me. I had recently gotten my tags renewed so I knew my tags were not the problem. In my mind, there was no reason for me to have been pulled over.

From the perspective of the police officers who stopped me, they were on the lookout for a black male driving a small silver two-door coupe. They did not know the exact make, model or year of the car. From their perspective, they were not looking to target me for some illicit reason. They were looking for a dangerous suspect who was sought for murder. They were on heightened alert because the person was probably still armed and dangerous since he was alleged to have just shot someone. They had to take every precaution. My silver two-door sports car fit as much of the description as the police officers had at the time they pulled me over. Again, please remember that oftentimes police officers are operating with limited information when they are investigating a crime. The reason for their stop may or may not have been a pretext for them to investigate me, but they had reason to be on alert for someone who might just look like me. The situation could have easily and rapidly escalated, but even in my annoyance and anger I followed some key suggestions that we outline below so you make it home alive after an encounter like mine.

As African-American men we are likely to encounter police in the context of a traffic stop at some point during our time as a driver. Please take a few things into consideration to help reduce the likelihood of being stopped by police at all. The obvious suggestion is to obey all traffic laws. We know how tempting it is to push the speed limit—after all I have been stopped several times for speed limit infractions. So do the best you can to comply with the speed limit. Even with speed limit enforcement many police officers will allow for a little leeway for speeding. If the speed limit is 25 mph and you are traveling 31 mph, you might not get pulled over. If, however, the speed limit is 25 mph and you are traveling 37 mph, you are more likely to be pulled over. We are not suggesting a way for you to speed and get away with it. We are just trying to make you aware of the practical considerations most officers will take into account when seeing a car traveling over the speed limit. If you are only 5 mph over the limit, you are less likely to be stopped. If you are 10 to 15 mph over the speed limit, you are more likely to be stopped. Just keep the "grace" speed of 5 mph in mind.

The other reason people are often pulled over is for vehicle defects. Police officers are responsible for public safety and it is not safe to have cars on the roads that have brake lights or head lights that don't work. So make sure that your vehicle has no defects before driving by looking at the following essentials and complying with these basic rules:

- Make sure headlights work—both of them
- Make sure your headlights are turned on at dusk
- Use your turn signals when turning or changing lanes
- Wear your seatbelt
- Some states prohibit use of cell phones or texting
- Make sure brake lights work—both of them
- Make sure your license plates are current
- Make sure you have a current inspection sticker
- Make sure nothing is hanging from your car

Paying attention to the above and addressing any known

problems can reduce the likelihood of you encountering police.

Recognizing that you can get pulled over for any of the items that we encourage you to inspect on your vehicle before driving, you are most likely to get pulled over by the police for a moving violation; most likely speeding. Whether it's speeding, running a red light, or running a stop sign, if you get pulled over by a police officer, the first thing to remember is to remain calm. Here are the other key points to remember:

- Do not get out of your car
- Do not make any sudden or dramatic moves
- Turn on interior lights of car—even in daytime
- Place both hands on the steering wheel so they are visible
- Tell the officer of every move you plan on making such as "I am reaching in my glove box to get my insurance card"
- Tell the officer "I am reaching for my wallet in my back pocket"

- Remember show the officer empathy and let him or her know you want them to feel safe through your calm and deliberate manner

Adrian and I both understand that your initial reaction during a stop may be one of annoyance, frustration, or even anger at what may seem like a constant harassment of black men. Before you start playing that story in your mind, take a deep breath and try to remain calm. Remember that your objective is to go home that day. If you were stopped for a valid reason, you now have information that can help you make the necessary adjustments to prevent future stops for that reason (e.g., defective brake lights, faulty headlight, etc.). Moreover, you may be able to make an argument in traffic court to have any fine that comes with your violation significantly reduced. The courts are always going to be your best venue to present your reason for the problem with your car or why you did not think your were speeding. Police officers hear excuses all day long and are not inclined to accept your reason although they might if you make your case in the appropriate manner to them and keep it brief.

Also keep in mind that police officers are often in the process of investigating reports of criminal activity. If you or your vehicle fit the description that police have, the police officers may use one of the vehicle defects mentioned above to stop you. They may stop you even without one of the vehicle defects above if you resemble the description of a suspect. Keep in mind my own encounter with police. In my mind, it was clearly unreasonable that I was surrounded by police officers with hands on their guns for having tinted windows. This did not make sense to me and angered me, but I kept the main objective in mind which was to leave that situation without being shot. As I later found out, the police officers had a valid reason for treating me the way they did. It was nothing personal. They had no intent to harass me. They wanted to catch a murder suspect and remove him from the streets. Keep in mind that there may be a valid reason that the police stop you and act in a manner that may not seem warranted to you.

Here is a recent example of an African-American man remaining calm and respectful as we outline in this book during his own encounter with police where he was being verbally abused by a rogue cop. Cincinnati Bengals Defensive Lineman Sam Montgomery was pulled over for a speeding violation driving 89 mph in a 55 mph zone in Laurens, South Carolina. South Carolina Highway Patrolman R.S. Salter verbally abused the NFL star who conducted himself appropriately during the whole encounter as we outlined above. The state trooper's patrol vehicle had a dash cam that recorded Trooper Salter's abusive conduct towards Mr. Montgomery. Trooper Salter also had previous written complaints in his employee file prior to pulling over the NFL player. Given his prior record which was documented through written complaints from other citizens and his misconduct in this incident, Trooper Salter got fired from his job and now has this stain on his record. It will be difficult for him to find employment in law enforcement ever again. Meanwhile, Sam Montgomery who remained calm, complied with each order, and did not resist was vindicated through another venue although not in the moment of the encounter, in spite of his traffic offense. Let Sam Montgomery's story serve as proof that reacting in the way that we outline in this book can and will have good results all the way around.[13] **Comply now and contest later.**

---

[13] http://www.wspa.com/story/26349145/trooper-fired-after-arrest-of-nfl-player-in-laurens-co

CHAPTER 6:
TERRY STOP ENCOUNTERS

PRACTICAL STEP NUMBER 4 FOR SURVIVING ENCOUNTERS WITH POLICE: WHEN DETAINED OR QUESTIONED BY POLICE REMEMBER PRACTICAL STEPS 2 AND 3

Police encounters that occur due to police having a reasonable suspicion of criminal activity are called a "Terry Stop." A "Terry Stop" is a brief detention by police on reasonable suspicion of criminal activity that is short of an arrest for probable cause.[14] A Terry Stop is what occurred when Eric Garner was approached by a plainclothes police officer to be questioned about selling untaxed cigarettes. As in that situation, many Terry Stops will occur outside of your vehicle or during a non-traffic encounter.

Most Terry Stops result from calls police receive about suspicious activity. Again, the police officers have

---

[14] See http://en.wikipedia.org/wiki/Terry_stop

limited information when they are responding to these calls. When you are stopped by a police officer for questioning the same rules that we described for traffic stops apply. First, remember to keep calm and do not make any sudden moves for any reason. Make sure you remember the following essential behaviors:

- Remain calm
- Do not make any sudden moves
- Inform the officer when you are reaching for your ID
- Do not escalate the situation by raising your voice or yelling
- Comply with the police officer(s) orders
- Do not argue
- Never physically resist a police officer
- Answer questions calmly
- Remember if the stop is invalid, the officer can be punished but not by you
- You can request to contact an attorney

Earlier in the book, I mentioned that I had two encounters with police officers that were not positive. One was discussed in Chapter 5 which involved the police stopping me in Washington, DC as they were searching for a murder suspect. That stop felt bad and was a negative interaction for the show of force for a seemingly minor vehicle defect. Upon further investigation, I took some comfort in learning that I was not being randomly harassed or treated illegally. The other negative incident that I recall happened when I was nine years old in my hometown of Hamilton, Ohio. We are sure that many of you can remember when you got your first off road bike and learned how to do a "wheelie hop" or "bunny hop." Adrian and I both had off road bikes with cool pads on different parts of the bicycle more for decoration than for protection. In the summer of 1978 I was riding my bike down Lane Street which is perpendicular to Hanover Street where I lived. As I was speeding down the sidewalk headed towards my home I tried to do a wheelie hop where I jumped my bike off the curb and into the street. As my bicycle landed in the street, I did not see a police cruiser driving down Lane Street about 5 to 10 yards away from me. I cut in front of the police cruiser which frightened me as I had not seen the car at all. I was startled when I heard the honk of a horn.

The police cruiser pulled to a stop and an officer yelled out of his window, "Hey, you get over here right now!" I slowly and sheepishly rode my bike over near the police cruiser and was terrified as to what might happen to me. Moreover, I was afraid because I was not supposed to be that far from my house. "Yes sir," I said. The officer sternly said, "You need to watch where you are riding and not cut across the street like that without looking. We almost ran you over and there would not have been anything in the street except a small, little black, nigger mark smashed in the street." I was stunned. I was so terrified because I did realize that I could have been run over and then I was mortified by the police officer's racial slur. I was so terrified that I simply said "Ok, I am sorry mister that I did that. I won't do it again." "Keep your ass out of the street boy," the officer yelled as they pulled off. Regrettably, some of you may have had similar harsh language used against you by a police officer. How did that make you feel? These injustices happen, but escalating them in the moment leads to results that are far worse than hurt feelings or bruised egos. By learning how to pick your battles with rogue police officers and more importantly by knowing when and where to fight with rogue police, you can regain some of your power that you may have felt taken from you as a youth or an adult.

My bike encounter was technically a Terry Stop. I was briefly detained by the police officers for "questioning" and I was suspected of a traffic infraction. If I had known about filing a complaint or reporting racial bias to the US Department of Justice, I would have reported that incident. This was obviously a bad encounter with police and it was in the late 1970s when diversity training was really missing. I now know many police officers on the Hamilton City Police Department some of whom are my former football teammates, classmates, and neighborhood friends. I know that they are fine people who will not conduct themselves in an unprofessional manner. Although I was frightened when the officers surrounded my car in Washington, DC with hands on their guns and just as I was as a nine year old riding my bike, I remained committed to reacting in the way that I have instructed you to do in this book. In any other encounter with police, I am committed to remaining calm, not making any sudden moves, and complying with all orders given by police. I always keep in mind that if the police officers are doing something wrong or illegal I have a way to get back at them. It may not be in that moment, but I do have avenues for making bad cops pay. So when you get pulled over by police or stopped for questioning, take a deep breath and remind yourself that whatever happens here is not final unless you escalate things to a point of violence where it could be final for you. By amplifying awareness about police misconduct through proper channels, you will have resources available to you no matter what course of action you take to seek retribution against a rogue police officer.

PRACTICAL STEP NUMBER 5 FOR SURVIVING ENCOUNTERS WITH POLICE: BE CAREFUL WHEN HOLDING A WEAPON OF ANY TYPE

Concealed Carry Permit: If you are an African-American man and have a concealed carry permit, here is a helpful tip for you as you legally carry your weapon: purchase and wear a concealed carry permit badge. When Adrian and I were growing up, many men in our neighborhood were hunters. My father was an avid hunter and owned several guns. Adrian carries a weapon as a police officer and even at times when he is off duty. After attending a gun show with a very politically conservative friend of mine who extolled the virtues of gun ownership and the Second Amendment, I actually took an interest in owning a hand gun. I was actually surprised at my reaction to attending a gun show and going to a shooting range. I had my own biases and preconceived notion of "what those type of people would be like" at a gun show or shooting range. I also had questions about the propriety of owning a handgun given violence in cities across the US and school shootings. One of the key benefits to opening your mind to another perspective or a different way of thinking is that you might actually learn something or find something that you really like. This was my own experience with my own path to gun ownership. What struck me about people at shooting ranges and gun shows to a lesser extent was their mutual respect for order and following the rules for gun ownership. I was amazed at how uniform everyone in a gun range was in following the rules of the range to make sure that everyone else felt safe and comfortable. If someone is careless in a gun range or fails to follow instructions, other people can get hurt. Most people are, therefore, hyper-vigilant about compliance with rules.

After receiving training and properly qualifying, I now hold a concealed carry permit in the Commonwealth of Virginia. I only use my weapon for sport (i.e., target shooting) at some local shooting ranges in my area. I do not carry my weapon unless I also have attached to my belt a "Concealed Carry Permit" badge. This is a badge that you can purchase at a gun store and it allows any law enforcement official to see a badge and makes them less likely to react in a hostile manner. In my state, police understand that there is both an open carry law and a concealed carry law. The police, therefore, may not necessarily be unnerved at the sight of someone with a weapon on their person or in the front seat of their car. I take this extra precaution because I want the police to see the badge whenever they see the gun on my hip. This is not intended to impersonate a police officer as the badge is clearly for a concealed carry permit. It does, however, force the police officer who might have a question to find out what the badge is. In the time that it takes to ascertain if I am a fellow law enforcement officer, a conversation can occur and concealed carry credentials can be produced. Make certain that you always have your concealed carry permit with you when carrying your weapon. If you have a concealed carry permit, you should purchase a concealed carry permit badge so if any questions are raised about you having a gun the law enforcement officer will see the badge and likely be slower to react to you in a hostile manner.

Toy Guns: If you are a young black boy and you want to purchase a toy gun or play with a toy gun, please make sure that any toy weapon you carry has a marking on it from the toy manufacturer identifying it as a toy gun. Federal law requires that toy guns have an orange plug in the barrel.[15] Also, if a police officer is in sight, please put the toy gun on the ground and do not point it at anyone. Tamir Rice held a toy gun in a Cleveland park and that gun did not have the orange plug on its barrel to identify it as a toy gun. Similarly, John Crawford was carrying a toy assault rifle that he pulled from a store shelf and was gunned down by police officers who thought the weapon was real. Be very careful in handling any toys that look like real weapons. Remember we said earlier that the police have to make their best guess based on the limited and often imperfect information they have. When you see police if you are holding a toy gun, put the gun down on the ground. The purpose of the toy is to play but be careful not to point the gun at anyone who is not playing with you or when in the presence of police.

---

[15] 15 USC § 5001(b)

CHAPTER 7:
THE COST, PROMISE, AND PAIN OF BEING A BLACK MAN IN AMERICA

PRACTICAL STEP NUMBER 6 FOR SURVIVING ENCOUNTERS WITH POLICE: REMEMBER OUR HISTORY AND OUR ABILITY TO OVERCOME CHALLENGES BASED ON RACE

Dr. Martin Luther King said that "violence is the language of the unheard." We want you to hear police and through education, advocacy and awareness work in the community, we want the police to hear you. Our hope is that with both sides being heard, violence can be reduced. Tragically, Ismaaiyl Brinsley shot and killed two New York City police officers on December 20, 2014 shortly after the grand jury verdicts not to indict police officers in the Eric Garner and Michael Brown cases. The killer posted rants days before on social media about avenging the deaths of unarmed black men killed by police and named both Eric Garner and Michael Brown.

In this uncivilized act, the killer did not bring justice for Garner or Brown. We are saddened for the loss of NYPD Officers Rafael Ramos and Wenjian Liu. Like, Dr. King we believe that unnecessary violence takes place when people do not hear each other. Black men are feeling unheard and frustrated but attacking police officers is never the solution. Moreover, we have provided detailed information for how you can be heard in the proper forum.

We don't need to recount every negative statistic that can be attached to black men and boys in the US. Black men have the highest homicide rate in the US. Black men have higher than average incarceration rates and high school dropout rates. Many black men feel overlooked and undervalued in both their professional and personal lives. Even with these major problems, there is hope. The United States elected an African-American as President. Notwithstanding all of the resistance President Barack Obama's Presidency has experienced some of which is no doubt rooted in racial animus and conscious and unconscious bias, black boys and men have reason to hope.

We challenge you to keep positive despite the challenges you face. We all have difficulties and no one is immune to facing life's major hurdles. What we hope to accomplish with this book is to share from our experiences as suspect, attorney, and police. We are African-American men who have successfully navigated careers and encounters with police and for Adrian Jackson encounters with the public as a police officer. Our hope is that this short and simple book will challenge black men to share this wisdom with other black men. We believe through sharing our experiences and our hopes things will get better. We know that there are black men out there who can tell you how to start a construction company and succeed. We know there are black men who can give you pointers on how to get through engineering school. We know black men who can coach younger black boys on how to stay in school and get a high school diploma. We know there are black men who have been in prison and are now members of society who make positive contributions. We hope that as a result of our sharing our experiences we can help prevent deaths of black men and boys in police encounters. We can and we will reverse the negative statistics often bantered about when discussing black men. We are in this together. Black and white men, white and black women, Asian and Hispanic, rich and poor--we are all in this together. As we work through the historic baggage that makes this particular form of injustice acutely aimed at black men and boys, we provide this framework as one in the many needed to end these unnecessary tragedies. In his famous Letter from the Birmingham Jail, Dr. Martin Luther King also wrote that "Injustice anywhere is a threat to justice everywhere. We are caught in an inescapable network of mutuality, tied in a single garment of destiny. Whatever affects one directly, affects all indirectly." Our prayer is that all of us understand this truth so that everyone leaves encounters with police safe, alive, and well.

ACKNOWLEDGEMENTS

We want to thank our family and friends who supported us as we wrote this book. We had a sense of urgency to get this project completed because we want to prevent senseless deaths of black men and boys today, tomorrow, and the next day. We especially want to thank those who provided their feedback on the book, editing, and suggestions. We want to thank Professor Phil Luther, Mukta Sambrani, Carolyn White, Vincent King, Sr., Doug Redd, Dr. Robert Rusbosin, Lonnie Sanders, Dr. Willie Jolley, Michel Daley, Patrick Gusman, Yeshi Zeleke and others who gave us help along the way with this journey. We want to especially thank those who started, led, supported, and sustained Israel Baptist Church where we met as young boys in a youth group. Finally, we want to thank the educational institutions that equipped us with critical thinking abilities and the opportunity to learn and grow: the Cincinnati Christian High School, the Ohio Peace Officer Training Academy, the University of Cincinnati (both Blue Ash and Main Campus), and the University of Virginia School of Law.

Eric C. Broyles is a Washington, DC based attorney and entrepreneur. Eric has been on both sides of the law as a juvenile delinquent in his hometown and as a lawyer at a large prestigious law firm, at AOL, Inc. and AOL Time Warner, Inc. He was also a judicial law clerk on the United States Court of Appeals for the Eleventh Circuit. He is passionate about sharing his wisdom and insights with youth and particularly those who like himself during his youth may believe that the odds are against them. Eric is a graduate of the University of Virginia School of Law where he served as Business Editor of the Virginia Journal of Law & Politics and is a *summa cum laude* graduate of the University of Cincinnati where he double majored in Marketing and Management. Eric has been invited to speak at many schools, prisons, churches, universities, and trade associations across the US.

Adrian Jackson is a 25 year veteran of an Ohio police department. He has been a Patrolman for his entire career working in some of the roughest parts of town. Adrian has also served as a Public School Resource Police Officer for 18 years in addition to his patrol work. He is active in his local community where he is a Board Member at the Serve City Homeless Shelter and is a member of the Israel Baptist Church where he has been a longtime member of the Choir. A noted vocalist, he is also a member of the gospel group Sons of Israel. Adrian is a graduate of Cincinnati Christian High School and the Ohio Peace Officer Training Academy. Adrian is also committed to helping youth and young people to achieve their fullest potential and that commitment is demonstrated through the many positive relationships he has in his community including with people he has previously arrested.

More information at:

www.survivethepolice.com

Made in the USA
Middletown, DE
29 July 2016